A YEAR OF QUESTIONS

A YEAR OF QUESTIONS

AJ Juarez

LOST VALLEY PRESS
HARDWICK, MA

In loving memory of my mother . . .
. . . to my brother Carlos
and Julie Murkette

. . . to the legacy of Pablo Neruda,
a man whose poetic works touched me deeply.
Mr. Neruda's books, Residence on Earth *and*
The Book of Questions *truly influenced my poetry*

. . . And to all my relations.

Many thanks to Bill Trembly, Jonathan Blake,
and Stephen Campiglio for their editorial support.

Table of Contents

April, May, June ....

July, August, September .... October again

October

November

December ....

Marking the Return

Marking the return
With words that camouflage
how it feels to be hugged by your niece
Or to kiss your mother on the forehead
knowing she will soon be dying.

Marking the return,
to the desert and the song I carry in me
Because of nativity

Again, we gather mesquite for the fire.
Again we sweat and sing to our Creator
and ask our old ones for their strength.
Again, we worship to the spirit of all our relations.
Again,
we are not
alone.

PABLO
For the Chilote and Mapuche people

Pablo // Neftali,
YOU POET, GHOST-MENTOR,
lover of creation, you!

Have you reincarnated as a leopard
Or an olive tree?

Is there another common denominator —
besides DNA —
between your killers and the oranges you loved?

Isn't CHILE
A delicious name for a country?

QUESTIONS FOR CATHOLICS

Does confession absolve a Catholic Priest
Of pedophilia?
Why is the nun so threatened by my question?

Does the POPE know
The joy of a tender kiss after making love?

BUDDHA BABY

Buddha baby,
do you know why I like you?
Did you know I trust your knowledge over
indulgences?

Ain't it great to have a fat imperfect deity?

New Math

What is 64 divided by .900 times
The speed of a broken heart?
If six of these and six of those
equal each other,
can we subtract ten of them and
eight of theirs to
again reach equilibrium?

If the total charge of the universe is zero,
what in creation is the obsession with
being number one?

With Animals

Wasn't it at 11:45 AM . . .
when the mole played with the moon?
Ain't you gonna mend the lizard's broken heart?
Again, frog, would you please stick out your tongue?
Aren't you interested in the butterfly's protein content?

TRULY VULGAR

What can be more vulgar then being unkind?

PEACE

When soldiers gather corpses,
do they think of their loved ones?
Tell me, why do we march to war
With such angelic music?

When we don't celebrate
our brief moment here,
do we forget the sun is finite?
Oh,
when will the dead sky stones smash the galaxies?
Before peace on earth?

WHY NOT ASK QUESTIONS
for Leonard Pelletier

Are those voices we are hearing
manic Quetzal screaming
For us to save the ozone?

The cry I bring back from the mountain,
can it be recycled?

Why not ask questions?
It's not about fear.

January

February

March....

LUAU

My sister's small dog wags its tail as he sees me approach.
I have eaten dogs like him
Under the blue Hawaiian night.
The taste of meat,
Delicious, at the luau.

SIERRA BUTTES CALIFORNIA
the line "like a katchina's cry" was the gift of Carlos Aceves

When I sat on those rocks,
Up there, on that mountain.
looking down over the pines,
all that I wanted was forgotten.
Sun shining, wind blowing
horizon's magic —
like a katchina's cry.

Tomasito's Poem

Knotted shoelace
child crying
my teeth and fingers help stop his
tears
Black shoelace
Untangled and retied.

HEAVENLY MOMENT

What did Miles play
for Bird when they first
met?

NEWTON'S INFLUENCE

If every action has an equal and opposite reaction and its effect,
what are we to do about climate change?

A dead turtle is left behind
by the tide.

WE

There. Again.
(This time in a letter).
WE.
I - You.
We
Love // You - I.
Here again.
We.

99 CENTS

99-cent burgers at
a fast food joint.
Caviar to a man with
his last two dollars
in his shirt pocket.

I-17

Free was traffic.
Cars speed by.
BANG!!!!
You dead.

Who taught us how to be so angry?

OPEN POETRY READING ~ WILLOW HOUSE

Care for lousy love, as in
". . . When you left me and my world . . . ah, love,
a rose I could not have."
I question your I, I,
I, as in
you.
Believe you masturbate with words // get off //
cum cuss you think
you've bathed in glorious feeling and
want to be understood. Go home!
Read Neruda. Read Gwen Brooks!

WOULD
For JPL

By nature,
she would undress slowly,
with grace and sensuality.

Watching her brush her teeth,
then her hair.
Observing how she washed her face
and applied moisturizer, I came
to understand the importance
of routines.

Her kisses //new paths,
lead me not toward heaven,
but toward the good earth.

POEM FOR JONATHAN

In a bar,
a TV set blares out a talk show.
We watch and
don't use our tongues.
Nostalgia for when,
over a few beers,
we would talk,
EVEN TO STRANGERS!

MUSIC LIVES

Brian
strung
like a fine tuned string
playing drums.
The sticks
switch on
his
being.
MUSIC LIVES!!!!!!!

WAS THAT HENRY WITH NANCY?

Was that Henry with Nancy?
Does Ron know they kiss under the fig tree?
In all her magnificence,
is she unhappy, or just horny?
Why should the cool autumn breeze mind infidelity?

SHE

Tongue
moving
just so.
Quivering body,
not a cliché,
she.

MOON WALTZ

Do you always smell this wonderful
when you're in bloom?
Your kiss,
besides being soft and gentle,
will it last?

Have you ever waltzed under a full moon
While naked and in love?

April

May

June....

AT THE PHOENIX, AZ PUBLIC LIBRARY

Looking out the window,
a man in a blue shirt sees a cubist stone sculpture.
Behind a tree a woman sleeps.
On the first floor of the library,
a huge bookshelf stands bearing three big signs
sternly confessing content:
"L FICTION M", "N FICTION R", "FILED BY AUTHOR".
Behind the bookshelf is a chair.

By noon, those of us without shelter have found our niche.
A man snores as a drunken woman meets a friend.
The time of day
Is given to others
as
the sun hotly bounces off the melting asphalt
on McDowell Avenue.

POEM FO' MICHAEL

"Why did so many heroin addicts die to give us great Jazz?"
asked Michael on his radio show. . . .

Since bent notes varying the scale gives us new tones,
Would anyone mind if Sun Ra's ghost bends the religious right
to see if they change their tune?

Look Mack, why do you mix politics with art?
Why can't you be cool Jazz,
(clear, vibrato-less, meticulously,
articulated music)?
YOU KNOW
The stuff off dreams!!!

WHO ASKED YOU, MOTHERFUCKER?!!!

LANGUAGE QUESTIONS

Who loaded all those synonyms and antonyms with meaning?
Say Scottie, why do you think elite erudite harlequins want to
kill language
with such strict definitions?
Haven't we proven that bad can mean good?
Tell me "professor," where is the homonym for
how it feels to be human?
We is we is how we is we how great we is we!
How you likes them apples, Mr. dissect the sentence dangling
participle,
irregular verbs, mechanized pseudo scientific, language scholar,
professor of futility?
Language is ORGANIC and LIVES MANY LIVES.
WORD!

WORD Up, ESE!
Word up!

CAVALCADE OF QUESTIONS
ON A SATURDAY AT 4 AM

What if the Demming New Mexico Rotarians
were divided when whole,
then multiplied by a rolling egg and immortalized by
the United States Bureau of Standards?

What are we to do with our dialogues on paper across a fading
blood line?

Don't I act wonderful as the man walking towards a red couch—
remote control gadget in hand?

Did I just see Michel cutting type from newspapers
and magazines
to compose his poems?

Aren't you tired of Wounded Eagle bragging
about his Sun Dance scars?

Tonight, how should I welcome sleep?

ON A PHOENIX, ARIZONA STREET

A young bald white man
walks toward my van.
He screams at a shadow I can't see.
"Look,
you bastard,
how could you reveal his investment
on the prior terrain he has known?
THIS IS HIS CAPITAL."

Closing his eyes, he speaks softly with himself.
I awkwardly
try to ignore him
as I take
pictures
of a Mexican
bird of fire
bush
flowering on the lawn
of a blue
boarded-up house.

Tire marks on wet soil,
left
zig-zag patterns,
left. . . . I went right
at the next corner.
A van turns a corner.
A traffic light turns green.
A bald white man screams again.

HE MIGHT NOT FEEL

So he might not feel like talking.
He snores with a copy of Isaac Bashevis Singer's
Friend of Kafka lying on his chest.
A radio plays a piece that sound like a selection
from Miles Davis's *Sketches of Spain*.
The hospital smells claim the moment.

I watch him stretch as he sleeps
and hope that if he wakes up he will welcomes words.
I was told his chance for
recovery is fifty/fifty
I wonder if this will be our last conversation.

He sleeps soundly while the I.V. solution
slowly enters his arm.
I count the drops of fluid leaving the I.V. bag.
Outside a sixth-floor window,
the gray sky is about to
cry.

AFTER THE CHANNEL 12 LATE NIGHT NEWSCAST

    ... then right then, came the moment when
all the nights converged. So there they were,
and no one can do anything about it.
The Germans speak, and Somalia speaks,
and the Libyans speak of hate, famine
    and war. Again, men lay familiar claims about right
and wrong and the arguments
    have understandably turned deadly. Again.
Again thousands did admire the
         enormous vision containing them.

    ... She said over a few beers,
"fuck the Jews and the Muslims.
In a few hundred years all life will be dead on this planet.
She started crying.
    Then sobbing.

    I looked at her and Stephen Campiglio's poem
about how death — murder or disease — is still death;
came screaming into my mind.
Her tears streamed down her face.
The bartender looked away.

    She said,
"I'm too drunk to think about life. Just fuck me."

July

August

September....

October, again

MONUMENTS

The legacy you've lived breathes
and pulsates:
13 children, 43 grandchildren, 8 great-grandchildren, and
countless others
who have been//touched
by your strength, your peaceful spirit.
To call you a matriarch would be irrelevant.
If you were a mountain or
a spawning fish,
if you were a flower or a cloud,
you would still humble us with your
lifetime.

Mother,
when you told me death did not frighten you
because you had never been afraid to live
you gave me the gift of understanding,
making our good-byes
farewells, and our
last moments together,
monuments to you.

MY GREATEST HONOR
Excerpts from letters

... Her death was not some magical journey on a spirit horse,
or white light from heaven.
Her death was not a hibiscus perfumed with her spirit.
Ornate, romantic language fails to truly mark her passing.

... My loss goes beyond the simple grief //non-acceptance
that may be relieved through primal screaming.

 ... my grief creates a void in which intimacy is lost.
Yes, intimacy.
An intimacy which goes far beyond the wondrous touch
of a loving, soothing hand,
caressing a forehead. The intimacy I'm missing is the faith
found in trusting someone without reservation.
It is the unconditional love and good will that sometimes bonds
a student with a mentor, a mother with her children,
a husband with a wife, a friend with friend.
I never realized
my faith in people was directly tied to her presence;
her love.

... I do not grieve her physical departure, after all,
she taught me that no one walks out of life alive.
No, it is not that simple.
What I grieve is the spiritual void in my life.
My greatest honor was to be her son.

... today I breathe sadness and time.
My sister Maty told us that in the old days it was said
that when a great spirit dies,
the creator gets so happy to welcome them
that he makes the rains come to honor the departed.
When my mother passed, it rained for six days.

... After, the rains, sitting with my sister Carmen,
we remind each other of mother's words,
"death is for the living, for they are left behind to grieve."

... Her death was not some magical journey on a spirit horse,
or white light from heaven.
Her death was not a hibiscus perfumed with her spirit.
Ornate, romantic language fails to truly mark her passing.
Her death is a monument to her life and the generations.

AN ODE TO THOSE WHO QUESTION

For my mother who taught me to question,
and for Stephen Hawking, whose book,
A Brief History of Time, *reminded me of questioning.*

I

The sky is clear and the moon is crescent.
A hot summer wind blows.
I've come to sit alone, to clear my mind
of thoughts which spin and weave,
shuffle and stray,
and say nothing.

I think of the billions of stars, out there,
in the known universe. My mind is fragmented and
fills itself with thoughts of Mayan Astronomer and interstellar
voyages of the Zapotec.
Thoughts of Newton's discovery of the spectrum of color close
up space?
found in a prism, of Hubble's
notion of the expanding universe, of Einstein — that Zionist
gift to humanity. My thoughts
boil and steam, clatter and squeak until the image of
Stephen Hawking
appears.
Professor Hawking,
sitting in his wheelchair, deformed, pained, struggling with
speech,
exploring, searching, living his life,
writing his *A Brief History of Time.*

His life full of meaning and significance, celebrating
questioning, becoming
part of the continuum covering the globe we call earth
kin to the Chinese
and their knowledge of rocketry
and to those Arabic thinkers
who gave us those powerful numerals we count.
Hawking, contributing, challenging, powerful.

The clear sky leads me toward the desert horizon
I've often called home.
I walk toward the horizon.
"My mother is dead, she taught me to question,"
I say to the stars as I tip an imaginary hat
to those who have asked.
"How does it work, this universe of ours?"

II
This clear windy night humbles me.
I, a grieving man in awe with creation.
I raise my hands to the cosmos
and cry.

IF

For my beloved wife and companion, DL

If, somehow, I could paint your laughter,
I would use yellows and pinks to illustrate your
thundering belly.
Lavender and oranges, with a bit of white, for
the pure joy seeded in your womb.
Your laughter would pass through bright desert yellows,
sprinkled
with a bit of turquoise and black,
making its way to the thorax, to
burst through
vocal chords of pastel rainbows, with a tingling sensation,
which would stay in a passion-red mouth,
long after the echoes
of your song
had died.

Then your eyes would shine with
clear kindness.

ABOUT THE POET

AJ Juarez is of the Ashiwee and Yeomen First Nations (Zuni and Yaqui). Poet, artist, writer, and musician, he is the founder of Noh Place Artists Cooperative and the former lead singer for The Ghost Shadows, a seminal Worcester band known for its unusual blending of Jazz, heavy metal, funk, Native American songs, and straight ahead rock. His Native flute musings can also be heard on John Zaganiacz's Virtual Equinox recordings.

As a student he coordinated the Poetry Center at Worcester State College and was a founding member of The Center for the Study of Human Rights. He was deeply involved in the No Nukes and Anti-Apartheid movements. He is a lifelong Jazz aficionado and a former Jazz host at WCUW (91.3 FM). His Jazz poetry and artwork can be seen on the jazzhistorydatabase.com website. His art work has also been used on book covers and as illustrations. In the 2018 exhibition, "A Forty Year Retrospective" at the MAP Gallery in Easthampton, MA, AJ and his visual arts mentor, Michel Duncan Merle, highlighted their collaboration as artists and poets.

AJ lives on a lake in Western Massachusetts.

Milton Keynes UK
Ingram Content Group UK Ltd.
UKHW012250290324
440241UK00004B/268

9 781935 874485